5 YEAR
Weather
DIARY

Belongs to:

Weather Tracker Ideas

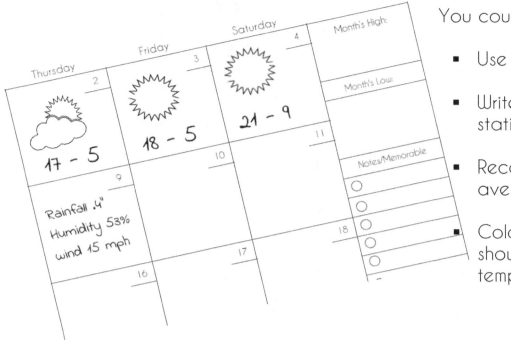

You could:

- Use Weather Symbols

- Write out selected statistics

- Record highs/lows or averages

- Color code each box showing average temperature

Useful Weather Symbols

Month   *Year*

Sunday	Monday	Tuesday	Wednesday

Thursday	Friday	Saturday	
			Month's High:
			Month's Low:
			Notes/Memorable
			○
			○
			○
			○
			○
			○
			○
			○
			○
			○
			○
			○

Month   Year

Sunday	Monday	Tuesday	Wednesday

Thursday	Friday	Saturday	
			Month's High:
			Month's Low:
			Notes/Memorable
			◯
			◯
			◯
			◯
			◯
			◯
			◯
			◯
			◯
			◯
			◯
			◯
			◯

Month   *Year*

Sunday	Monday	Tuesday	Wednesday

Thursday	Friday	Saturday	
			Month's High:
			Month's Low:
			Notes/Memorable
			○
			○
			○
			○
			○
			○
			○
			○
			○
			○
			○

Month   Year

Sunday	Monday	Tuesday	Wednesday

Thursday	Friday	Saturday	
			Month's High:
			Month's Low:
			Notes/Memorable
			○
			○
			○
			○
			○
			○
			○
			○
			○
			○
			○
			○

Month   Year

Sunday	Monday	Tuesday	Wednesday

Thursday	Friday	Saturday	
			Month's High:
			Month's Low:
			Notes/Memorable
			○
			○
			○
			○
			○
			○
			○
			○
			○
			○
			○
			○

Month   *Year*

Sunday	Monday	Tuesday	Wednesday

Thursday	Friday	Saturday	
			Month's High:
			Month's Low:
			Notes/Memorable
			○
			○
			○
			○
			○
			○
			○
			○
			○
			○
			○
			○

Month

Year

Sunday	Monday	Tuesday	Wednesday

Thursday	Friday	Saturday	
			Month's High:
			Month's Low:
			Notes/Memorable
			◯
			◯
			◯
			◯
			◯
			◯
			◯
			◯
			◯
			◯
			◯
			◯

Month *Year*

Sunday	Monday	Tuesday	Wednesday

Thursday	Friday	Saturday	
			Month's High:
			Month's Low:
			Notes/Memorable
			○
			○
			○
			○
			○
			○
			○
			○
			○
			○
			○
			○

Month   Year

Sunday	Monday	Tuesday	Wednesday

Thursday	Friday	Saturday	
			Month's High:
			Month's Low:
			Notes/Memorable
			○
			○
			○
			○
			○
			○
			○
			○
			○
			○
			○
			○

Month

Year

Sunday	Monday	Tuesday	Wednesday

Thursday	Friday	Saturday	

			Month's High:
			Month's Low:
			Notes/Memorable
			○
			○
			○
			○
			○
			○
			○
			○
			○
			○
			○
			○
			○

Month

Year

Sunday	Monday	Tuesday	Wednesday

Thursday	Friday	Saturday	
			Month's High:
			Month's Low:
			Notes/Memorable
			○
			○
			○
			○
			○
			○
			○
			○
			○
			○
			○
			○

Month   *Year*

Sunday	Monday	Tuesday	Wednesday

Thursday	Friday	Saturday	
			Month's High:
			Month's Low:
			Notes/Memorable
			◯
			◯
			◯
			◯
			◯
			◯
			◯
			◯
			◯
			◯
			◯
			◯

Month

Year

Sunday	Monday	Tuesday	Wednesday

Thursday	Friday	Saturday	
			Month's High:
			Month's Low:
			Notes/Memorable
			◯
			◯
			◯
			◯
			◯
			◯
			◯
			◯
			◯
			◯
			◯
			◯

Month _____ *Year* _____

Sunday	Monday	Tuesday	Wednesday

Thursday	Friday	Saturday	
			Month's High:
			Month's Low:
			Notes/Memorable
			◯
			◯
			◯
			◯
			◯
			◯
			◯
			◯
			◯
			◯
			◯
			◯

Month

Year

Sunday	Monday	Tuesday	Wednesday

Thursday	Friday	Saturday	
			Month's High:
			Month's Low:
			Notes/Memorable
			○
			○
			○
			○
			○
			○
			○
			○
			○
			○
			○
			○

Month   *Year*

Sunday	Monday	Tuesday	Wednesday

Thursday	Friday	Saturday	
			Month's High:
			Month's Low:
			Notes/Memorable
			○
			○
			○
			○
			○
			○
			○
			○
			○
			○
			○
			○

Month   Year

Sunday	Monday	Tuesday	Wednesday

Thursday	Friday	Saturday	
			Month's High:
			Month's Low:
			Notes/Memorable
			○
			○
			○
			○
			○
			○
			○
			○
			○
			○
			○
			○

Month   Year

Sunday	Monday	Tuesday	Wednesday

Thursday	Friday	Saturday	
			Month's High:
			Month's Low:
			Notes/Memorable
			○
			○
			○
			○
			○
			○
			○
			○
			○
			○
			○
			○

Month

Year

Sunday	Monday	Tuesday	Wednesday

Thursday	Friday	Saturday	
			Month's High:
			Month's Low:
			Notes/Memorable
			○
			○
			○
			○
			○
			○
			○
			○
			○
			○
			○
			○

Month   *Year*

Sunday	Monday	Tuesday	Wednesday

Thursday	Friday	Saturday	
			Month's High:
			Month's Low:
			Notes/Memorable
			○
			○
			○
			○
			○
			○
			○
			○
			○
			○
			○
			○

Month   Year

Sunday	Monday	Tuesday	Wednesday

Thursday	Friday	Saturday	
			Month's High:
			Month's Low:
			Notes/Memorable
			○
			○
			○
			○
			○
			○
			○
			○
			○
			○
			○
			○

Month

Year

Sunday	Monday	Tuesday	Wednesday

Thursday	Friday	Saturday	
			Month's High:
			Month's Low:
			Notes/Memorable
			◯
			◯
			◯
			◯
			◯
			◯
			◯
			◯
			◯
			◯
			◯
			◯

Month   Year

Sunday	Monday	Tuesday	Wednesday

Thursday	Friday	Saturday	
			Month's High:
			Month's Low:
			Notes/Memorable
			◯
			◯
			◯
			◯
			◯
			◯
			◯
			◯
			◯
			◯
			◯
			◯

Month   *Year*

Sunday	Monday	Tuesday	Wednesday

Thursday	Friday	Saturday	
			Month's High:
			Month's Low:
			Notes/Memorable
			◯
			◯
			◯
			◯
			◯
			◯
			◯
			◯
			◯
			◯
			◯

Month

Year

Sunday	Monday	Tuesday	Wednesday

Thursday	Friday	Saturday	
			Month's High:
			Month's Low:
			Notes/Memorable
			○
			○
			○
			○
			○
			○
			○
			○
			○
			○
			○

Month

Year

Sunday	Monday	Tuesday	Wednesday

Thursday	Friday	Saturday	
			Month's High:
			Month's Low:
			Notes/Memorable
			○
			○
			○
			○
			○
			○
			○
			○
			○
			○
			○
			○

Month

Year

Sunday	Monday	Tuesday	Wednesday

Thursday	Friday	Saturday	
			Month's High:
			Month's Low:
			Notes/Memorable
			◯
			◯
			◯
			◯
			◯
			◯
			◯
			◯
			◯
			◯
			◯
			◯

Month   *Year*

Sunday	Monday	Tuesday	Wednesday

Thursday	Friday	Saturday	
			Month's High:
			Month's Low:
			Notes/Memorable
			○
			○
			○
			○
			○
			○
			○
			○
			○
			○
			○
			○

Month

Year

Sunday	Monday	Tuesday	Wednesday

Thursday	Friday	Saturday	
			Month's High:
			Month's Low:
			Notes/Memorable
			○
			○
			○
			○
			○
			○
			○
			○
			○
			○
			○
			○

Month
Year

Sunday	Monday	Tuesday	Wednesday

Thursday	Friday	Saturday	
			Month's High:
			Month's Low:
			Notes/Memorable
			○
			○
			○
			○
			○
			○
			○
			○
			○
			○
			○
			○

Month   Year

Sunday	Monday	Tuesday	Wednesday

Thursday	Friday	Saturday	
			Month's High:
			Month's Low:
			Notes/Memorable
			○
			○
			○
			○
			○
			○
			○
			○
			○
			○
			○
			○

Month

Year

Sunday	Monday	Tuesday	Wednesday

Thursday	Friday	Saturday	
			Month's High:
			Month's Low:
			Notes/Memorable
			○
			○
			○
			○
			○
			○
			○
			○
			○
			○
			○
			○

Month   Year

Sunday	Monday	Tuesday	Wednesday

Thursday	Friday	Saturday	
			Month's High:
			Month's Low:
			Notes/Memorable
			◯
			◯
			◯
			◯
			◯
			◯
			◯
			◯
			◯
			◯
			◯
			◯
			◯

Month   *Year*

Sunday	Monday	Tuesday	Wednesday

Thursday	Friday	Saturday	
			Month's High:
			Month's Low:
			Notes/Memorable
			◯
			◯
			◯
			◯
			◯
			◯
			◯
			◯
			◯
			◯
			◯

Month

Year

Sunday	Monday	Tuesday	Wednesday

Thursday	Friday	Saturday	
			Month's High:
			Month's Low:
			Notes/Memorable
			○
			○
			○
			○
			○
			○
			○
			○
			○
			○
			○
			○

Month   *Year*

Sunday	Monday	Tuesday	Wednesday

Thursday	Friday	Saturday	
			Month's High:
			Month's Low:
			Notes/Memorable
			◯
			◯
			◯
			◯
			◯
			◯
			◯
			◯
			◯
			◯
			◯

Month   # Year

	Sunday	Monday	Tuesday	Wednesday

Thursday	Friday	Saturday	
			Month's High:
			Month's Low:
			Notes/Memorable
			◯
			◯
			◯
			◯
			◯
			◯
			◯
			◯
			◯
			◯
			◯
			◯

Month

Year

Sunday	Monday	Tuesday	Wednesday

Thursday	Friday	Saturday	
			Month's High:
			Month's Low:
			Notes/Memorable
			○
			○
			○
			○
			○
			○
			○
			○
			○
			○
			○
			○

Month

Year

Sunday	Monday	Tuesday	Wednesday

Thursday	Friday	Saturday	
			Month's High:
			Month's Low:
			Notes/Memorable
			○
			○
			○
			○
			○
			○
			○
			○
			○
			○
			○
			○

Month   *Year*

Sunday	Monday	Tuesday	Wednesday

Thursday	Friday	Saturday	
			Month's High:
			Month's Low:
			Notes/Memorable
			○
			○
			○
			○
			○
			○
			○
			○
			○
			○
			○
			○

Month   *Year*

Sunday	Monday	Tuesday	Wednesday

Thursday	Friday	Saturday	
			Month's High:
			Month's Low:
			Notes/Memorable
			○
			○
			○
			○
			○
			○
			○
			○
			○
			○
			○
			○

Month

Year

Sunday	Monday	Tuesday	Wednesday

Thursday	Friday	Saturday	
			Month's High:
			Month's Low:
			Notes/Memorable
			◯
			◯
			◯
			◯
			◯
			◯
			◯
			◯
			◯
			◯
			◯
			◯

Month   *Year*

Sunday	Monday	Tuesday	Wednesday

Thursday	Friday	Saturday	
			Month's High:
			Month's Low:
			Notes/Memorable
			◯
			◯
			◯
			◯
			◯
			◯
			◯
			◯
			◯
			◯
			◯
			◯

Month

Year

Sunday	Monday	Tuesday	Wednesday

Thursday	Friday	Saturday	
			Month's High:
			Month's Low:
			Notes/Memorable
			○
			○
			○
			○
			○
			○
			○
			○
			○
			○
			○
			○

Month
Year

Sunday	Monday	Tuesday	Wednesday

Thursday	Friday	Saturday	
			Month's High:
			Month's Low:
			Notes/Memorable
			◯
			◯
			◯
			◯
			◯
			◯
			◯
			◯
			◯
			◯
			◯
			◯

Month   Year

Sunday	Monday	Tuesday	Wednesday

Thursday	Friday	Saturday	
			Month's High:
			Month's Low:
			Notes/Memorable
			○
			○
			○
			○
			○
			○
			○
			○
			○
			○
			○
			○

Month   *Year*

Sunday	Monday	Tuesday	Wednesday

Thursday	Friday	Saturday	
			Month's High:
			Month's Low:
			Notes/Memorable
			○
			○
			○
			○
			○
			○
			○
			○
			○
			○
			○
			○

Month

Year

Sunday	Monday	Tuesday	Wednesday

Thursday	Friday	Saturday	
			Month's High:
			Month's Low:
			Notes/Memorable
			◯
			◯
			◯
			◯
			◯
			◯
			◯
			◯
			◯
			◯
			◯
			◯

Month   *Year*

Sunday	Monday	Tuesday	Wednesday

Thursday	Friday	Saturday	
			Month's High:
			Month's Low:
			Notes/Memorable
			◯
			◯
			◯
			◯
			◯
			◯
			◯
			◯
			◯
			◯
			◯
			◯

Month   *Year*

Sunday	Monday	Tuesday	Wednesday

Thursday	Friday	Saturday	
			Month's High:
			Month's Low:
			Notes/Memorable
			○
			○
			○
			○
			○
			○
			○
			○
			○
			○
			○
			○

Month   Year

Sunday	Monday	Tuesday	Wednesday

Thursday	Friday	Saturday	
			Month's High:
			Month's Low:
			Notes/Memorable
			○
			○
			○
			○
			○
			○
			○
			○
			○
			○
			○
			○

Month   Year

Sunday	Monday	Tuesday	Wednesday

Thursday	Friday	Saturday	
			Month's High:
			Month's Low:
			Notes/Memorable
			○
			○
			○
			○
			○
			○
			○
			○
			○
			○
			○

Month   *Year*

Sunday	Monday	Tuesday	Wednesday

Thursday	Friday	Saturday	
			Month's High:
			Month's Low:
			Notes/Memorable
			○
			○
			○
			○
			○
			○
			○
			○
			○
			○
			○
			○

Month   *Year*

Sunday	Monday	Tuesday	Wednesday

Thursday	Friday	Saturday	
			Month's High:
			Month's Low:
			Notes/Memorable
			○
			○
			○
			○
			○
			○
			○
			○
			○
			○
			○

Month   Year

Sunday	Monday	Tuesday	Wednesday

Thursday	Friday	Saturday	
			Month's High:
			Month's Low:
			Notes/Memorable
			○
			○
			○
			○
			○
			○
			○
			○
			○
			○
			○
			○

Month   _Year_

Sunday	Monday	Tuesday	Wednesday

Thursday	Friday	Saturday	
			Month's High:
			Month's Low:
			Notes/Memorable
			◯
			◯
			◯
			◯
			◯
			◯
			◯
			◯
			◯
			◯
			◯
			◯

Month

Year

Sunday	Monday	Tuesday	Wednesday

Thursday	Friday	Saturday	
			Month's High:
			Month's Low:
			Notes/Memorable
			○
			○
			○
			○
			○
			○
			○
			○
			○
			○
			○
			○

Month   Year

Sunday	Monday	Tuesday	Wednesday

Thursday	Friday	Saturday	
			Month's High:
			Month's Low:
			Notes/Memorable
			○
			○
			○
			○
			○
			○
			○
			○
			○
			○
			○
			○

Month   Year

Sunday	Monday	Tuesday	Wednesday

Thursday	Friday	Saturday	
			Month's High:
			Month's Low:
			Notes/Memorable
			○
			○
			○
			○
			○
			○
			○
			○
			○
			○
			○
			○

Month   Year

Sunday	Monday	Tuesday	Wednesday

Thursday	Friday	Saturday	
			Month's High:
			Month's Low:
			Notes/Memorable
			◯
			◯
			◯
			◯
			◯
			◯
			◯
			◯
			◯
			◯
			◯
			◯

Made in the USA
Middletown, DE
13 August 2023

36647527R00071